BOYNTON BEACH CITY LIBRARY

SO-BSZ-526

Sharpen Your Writing Skills

SHARPEN YOUR
Story or Narrative
Writing Skills

Titles in the **Sharpen Your Writing Skills** series:

Sharpen Your Business Letter Writing Skills

Library Ed. ISBN: 978-0-7660-3972-8
Paperback ISBN: 978-1-59845-377-5

Sharpen Your Essay Writing Skills

Library Ed. ISBN: 978-0-7660-3903-2
Paperback ISBN: 978-1-59845-342-3

Sharpen Your Report Writing Skills

Library Ed. ISBN: 978-0-7660-3905-6
Paperback ISBN: 978-1-59845-338-6

Sharpen Your Story Or Narrative Writing Skills

Library Ed. ISBN: 978-0-7660-3901-8
Paperback ISBN: 978-1-59845-340-9

Sharpen Your Debate And Speech Writing Skills

Library Ed. ISBN: 978-0-7660-3904-9
Paperback ISBN: 978-1-59845-341-6

Sharpen Your Good Grammar Skills

Library Ed. ISBN: 978-0-7660-3902-5
Paperback ISBN: 978-1-59845-339-3

Sharpen Your Writing Skills

SHARPEN YOUR
Story or Narrative
Writing Skills

Jennifer Rozines Roy

Enslow Publishers, Inc.
40 Industrial Road
Box 398
Berkeley Heights, NJ 07922
USA

http://www.enslow.com

Copyright © 2012 by Jennifer Rozines Roy

All rights reserved.

No part of this book may be reproduced by any means
without the written permission of the publisher.

Original edition published as *You Can Write A Story Or Narrative* in 2003.

Library of Congress Cataloging-in-Publication Data

Roy, Jennifer Rozines, 1967–
    Sharpen Your Story Or Narrative Writing Skills / Jennifer Rozines Roy.
        p. cm. — (Sharpen your writing skills)
    Includes index.
    Summary: "Learn the parts of a narrative, the steps in the writing process, and
writing examples and ideas"—Provided by publisher.
    ISBN 978-0-7660-3901-8
    1. Authorship—Juvenile literature. 2. Narration (Rhetoric)—Juvenile literature.
3. Report writing—Juvenile literature. I. Title.
    PN159.R67 2011
    808'.02—dc22
    2010053471

Paperback ISBN: 978-1-59845-340-9

Printed in China

052011 Leo Paper Group, Heshan City, Guangdong, China

10 9 8 7 6 5 4 3 2 1

To Our Readers: We have done our best to make sure all Internet addresses in this
book were active and appropriate when we went to press. However, the author and
the publisher have no control over and assume no liability for the material available
on those Internet sites or on other Web sites they may link to. Any comments or
suggestions can be sent by e-mail to comments@enslow.com or to the address on
the back cover.

Illustration Credits: Enslow Publishers, Inc.

Cover Illustration: Shutterstock.com

Table of Contents

Chapter One

You Can Write a Narrative

"Tell me a story!"
From the time you were very little, you have known what a good story is. A story tells a tale that keeps you interested. It has characters you care about. And it uses words in ways that capture your imagination. When you were small, you probably did not think about the way the story was written. You just enjoyed it.

Now that you are older, you realize that stories do not just appear out of thin air. They are invented by people who decided that they have something interesting to say. As a student writer, it is your turn to tell the story. But how do you find something worth writing about? How do you put together words and sentences in just the right way? And how do you know if what you have written is any good? This book can help.

What Is a Narrative?

Narrative is another word for story. Narrative writing communicates the writer's ideas in a creative way. The story may be a realistic account with true events and real people. This is known as nonfiction. Or it may be made-up, featuring characters or events that are not real. This is called fiction. The type of narrative you choose to write depends on the story that you have to tell and the way you want to tell it.

> Once upon a time, there was a narrative. It had a beginning, middle, and end, and it was fun to read. . . .

All narratives have certain features in common. They each have a beginning, middle, and end. They contain story elements such as plot, setting, conflict, character, and theme. Good narratives use these elements to make the story come alive.

You Can Do It!

Writing a narrative is not always simple. Unfortunately, the right words do not just fall from your brain onto the paper. The writing process involves many stages—planning, organizing, drafting, revising, and publishing. While narrative writing is certainly creative and imaginative, it also requires hard work and specific skills to be done well.

Why write a narrative?

Writing can be challenging. It can be frustrating. It is hard work. So why do so many people write narratives?

1. **To tell a story.** Writing down an important event, an invented tale, or an ordinary moment captures your thoughts and allows you to share them with others.

2. **To become better thinkers and learners.** Writing gives you the chance to learn about new things and explore different ideas.

3. **To have fun.** Writing can transport you to a different time and place—one that you create.

4. **To express emotion.** Writing can help people deal with all kinds of emotions—anger, sadness, joy, and confusion. People often feel better when they write about their feelings.

5. **To excel in school.** The more you write, the better you will get. Better writing can lead to improved performance in all your classes.

6. **To become rich and famous.** Okay, it's true—very few writers ever become rich or famous. But it does happen! And thousands of others earn a successful living from writing—or simply enjoy writing on the side.

However difficult the process may seem at times, the rewards make narrative writing worthwhile. Writing can be a lot of fun. It allows you to express yourself and to be original. And when all the work is done, you can share it with others. As the author of a story, your efforts get recognized, and when you know your writing has touched somebody, it gives you a good feeling.

You *can* write a narrative! First, though, there are some things you need to know. In the following chapters you will learn all the parts of a narrative. You will learn the steps of the writing process. You will also find examples and ideas to spark your imagination. Writing a successful narrative will give you a sense of pride and accomplishment.

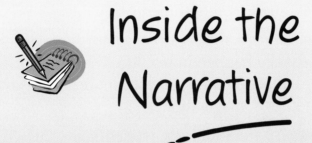

Chapter Two

Inside the Narrative

There are three types of narratives: fiction, nonfiction, and personal. *Fiction narratives* are not real but often express the truth. They come from the writer's imagination, though they may be based on realistic events. *Nonfiction narratives* describe real people and events. They are true stories. *Personal narratives* are based on the experiences of the author.

The Genres

A genre (pronounced "jhan-ra") is a category of writing with certain characteristics. Narrative writing is a major literary genre, with lots of "mini-genres" within it. Here are a few of them:

Adventures have lots of action. The characters must face challenges, often life-threatening, and overcome obstacles in their way.

Animal stories are about animals. They may be realistic, or they may act and speak like humans.

Biographies tell the true story of a person's life. They share facts about the subject's personality, struggles, and accomplishments.

Fantasies are about extraordinary experiences that do not usually happen in real life. They may include creatures, places, events, and inventions that exist only in the author's imagination.

Folktales are traditional stories handed down from generation to generation. They contain memorable characters (animal or human). Fables are like folktales, but they usually teach a lesson.

Historical narratives take place in the past. They may be real or imagined stories, but they are based on people, places, or events that existed before the present time.

Humorous narratives are funny. They may also have serious parts to them, but the main goal is to make the reader laugh through the amusing person-alities, conflicts, and actions of the characters.

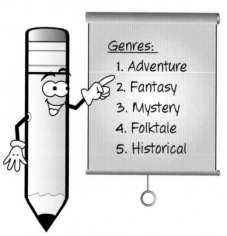

Genres:
1. Adventure
2. Fantasy
3. Mystery
4. Folktale
5. Historical

Multicultural narratives focus on a different culture or ethnic group. They

Examples of narratives:

Here are some examples of narratives you may be familiar with, along with the type and genre of each.

Harry Potter and the Sorcerer's Stone by J. K. Rowling—fantasy

A Wrinkle in Time by Madeleine L'Engle—science fiction

Dicey's Song by Cynthia Voight—fiction, realistic

Hatchet by Gary Paulsen—fiction, adventure

Dragonwings by Lawrence Yep—fiction, multicultural

Fireflies! by Julius Brinckloe—nonfiction, animal

Where Do You Think You Are Going, Christopher Columbus? by Jean Fritz—nonfiction, historical, biography

A Very Young Skater by Jill Krementz—nonfiction, sports

Redwall by Brian Jacques—fantasy, animal

Superfudge by Judy Blume—fiction, humorous

tell about places and people that may not be familiar to every reader.

Mysteries have a puzzle or secret that needs to be discovered or explained. The main character usually attempts to gather clues that will "unlock" the mystery.

Realistic narratives are about people, places, and events that could be true. The story is believable and actually could happen.

Romances spotlight love and relationships, but the "road to happiness" is usually bumpy.

Science fiction uses ideas from science and technology to create stories about the future or life on other planets. The events in the story probably couldn't happen now, but they may come true someday.

Sports narratives are about athletes or sporting events. Great sports stories make readers feel like they are watching the action from a front-row seat or through the eyes of the athletes themselves.

Which genres have you read? Which interest you most? Writers usually choose to write narratives in the genre or genres they find enjoyable. Of course, as a student writer, you may be given assignments in different genres. This is a good opportunity to explore subjects and ideas you might not ordinarily consider. Experimenting with various genres can help you become a strong narrative writer. The more practice you get with different kinds of writing, the more skilled you will become.

Parts of a Narrative

All narratives have three main parts—a beginning, middle, and ending. The beginning is important. It must be interesting enough to capture the readers' attention so that they want to read more. The beginning introduces the subject of the narrative and sets the mood and direction.

The body is the biggest section of the narrative.

The middle of a narrative is called the main body. This section is the big one. It contains the ideas, facts, and events that make up most of the story.

The ending wraps up the story. It can satisfy the reader by solving a problem or answering a question. It can offer a surprise twist. It can end "happily ever after" or even "unhappily ever after."

The Plot

The plot is the series of events in a narrative. The plot tells what happens in the story. A narrative plot most commonly has a certain order that begins with the *exposition*. This is the beginning part that introduces the people, place, and problem in the story. Next comes the *rising action*. The characters experience increasing complications in the problem or problems that they try to overcome. The *climax* is the high point of the story. It is the most exciting and intense moment. After the climax, the story quiets down. This is the *falling action*, where the characters deal with the effects of the climax. Finally, the story is brought to a

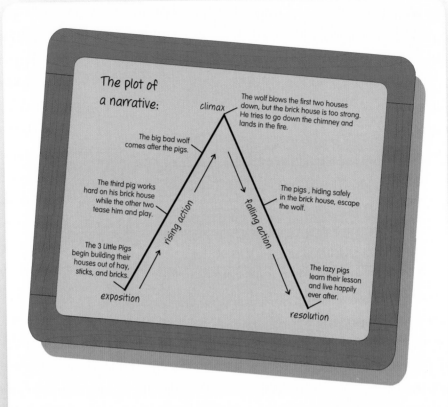

The plot of a narrative:

exposition

The 3 Little Pigs begin building their houses out of hay, sticks, and bricks.

The third pig works hard on his brick house while the other two tease him and play.

rising action

The big bad wolf comes after the pigs.

climax

The wolf blows the first two houses down, but the brick house is too strong. He tries to go down the chimney and lands in the fire.

falling action

The pigs , hiding safely in the brick house, escape the wolf.

The lazy pigs learn their lesson and live happily ever after.

resolution

close with the *resolution*. The resolution, also called the *denouement*, is the ending of the narrative.

The Setting

The setting is the *time* and *place* in which the story occurs. The setting tells where and when the action happened. When writing a narrative, you could include descriptions of the environment so that the readers can see it in their minds.

Think about your favorite story. Where does it happen? How did the author use words to make you remember that setting? The words that describe the setting are called *sensory details*. They are essential to helping the writer and reader get into the story. Sensory details share the way the place looks, sounds, smells, and feels. For example, your favorite beach could be described in this way: "The salty breeze was warm and gentle against my sunburned cheeks. It blew ripples across the clear, blue water. I dug my toes into the gritty sand and watched as a fat seagull dove for its breakfast on the shore."

Use your imagination when writing about the setting. Do not just come straight out and tell your reader, "It takes place on a beach. Seagulls fly through the air." Be creative and show the images through sensory details.

One caution—don't spend *too* much time on the setting. A narrative can get bogged down if the action does not move forward. An effective setting forms a background that makes the reader feel that he or she is there, while keeping the story interesting. You can also sprinkle details about the setting throughout the story, rather than overloading the beginning with a complete description.

I'm proud to be the protagonist! I'm learning about narratives as this book proceeds!

The Characters

Who are the characters in a narrative? They are the people

Character map:

One characterization tool is the character map. It allows you to see the different traits of your characters and then use those details in your narrative.

Here is an example of a character map for Calvin O'Keefe, a supporting character in a fiction narrative—Madeleine L'Engle's book *A Wrinkle in Time*. Notice how specific descriptive details give you a good picture of this person.

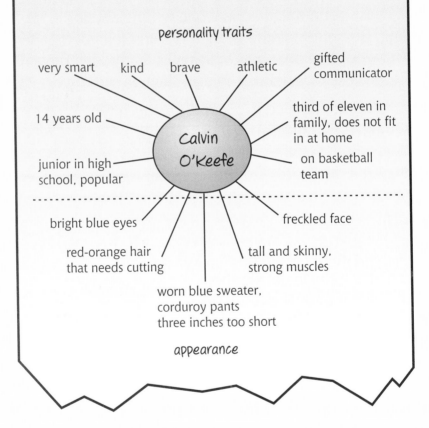

personality traits

very smart   kind   brave   athletic   gifted communicator

14 years old

third of eleven in family, does not fit in at home

Calvin O'Keefe

junior in high school, popular

on basketball team

bright blue eyes

freckled face

red-orange hair that needs cutting

tall and skinny, strong muscles

worn blue sweater, corduroy pants three inches too short

appearance

that the reader learns to care about. A good narrative contains characters who seem real and whose personalities draw readers into the story. Just like real people, they have strengths and weaknesses and specific personalities.

The main character is known as the *protagonist*. The protagonist is at the center of the story, and the reader usually roots for him or her. The protagonist faces the story's problem and usually learns and grows along the way. The other characters in the narrative are called *secondary characters*. They may help the protagonist or get in his or her way.

In a fiction narrative, the characters are made up but can be based on real people. Some narratives, like science fiction and fantasies, use animals or invented creatures as characters. The characters in nonfiction narratives are real. They may be alive or dead, but at one time they did exist. In a personal narrative, secondary characters are people you have known. They may be friends, family members, acquaintances, or even enemies—anyone who contributed to your story. The main character in a personal narrative is you.

Think about your favorite characters in narratives you have enjoyed. What did they look like? What were their personalities like? What were their likes and dislikes? The way to create memorable characters is to get to know them and to write about them as if they were real.

Chapter Three

Making It More Interesting

You have learned about some of the elements in a narrative. However, there are many other elements that are not as obvious at first. Yet these elements can help make a narrative more engaging.

Conflict

Conflict is the problem or struggle in a story. The character tries to achieve a goal, but something is standing in his or her way. Conflict does not need to mean fighting or violence. It is two forces that work against each other. While the protagonist in a story is the main character, the character or force that causes a conflict with the protagonist is called the *antagonist*.

Without conflict the story would be boring. What makes a story enticing is when characters face a challenge. The conflict provides action and suspense. When characters run up against a conflict, we want to know what happens. How do the characters try to overcome the obstacle? Do they face the challenge? Do they triumph? Or do they fail? How the conflict is worked out, or resolved, gives the narrative a conclusion.

Kinds of Conflict

Different kinds of conflict help create tension in a narrative. Some of the most common kinds are:

1. Person vs. Person

A character has a problem with one or more of the other characters. For example:

- A girl argues with her brother over which television show to watch.
- A baby-sitter tries to get the mischievous twins to go to bed.

2. Person vs. Society

A character has a problem with something in society, such as a rule, the law, or the accepted way of doing something. For example:

- A boy protests a playground being torn down to make a parking lot.
- Rosa Parks refuses to move to the back of the bus.

3. Person vs. Nature

A character has a problem with the environment. For example:

- A girl walks out of the salon with her new hairstyle, and it starts to rain.
- A skier hears the rumble of an avalanche.

4. Person vs. Self

A character has a problem deciding what to do in a particular situation. For example:

- A boy sees a spaceship with an alien beckoning him to come on board.
- A girl cannot decide if she wants to invite the new girl to her sleepover.

Help! I'm having a "person vs. nature" conflict!

I'll give you a hand!

A conflict can result in a situation that evokes different feelings: humor, sadness, drama, happiness. Think of your favorite story. What is the conflict? Who is involved in the conflict?

All personal narratives should have at least one conflict. After all, nobody lives a life without a problem or a challenge. There often is more than one conflict in a story. Some narratives include both major and minor conflicts. Have you ever started reading a book and then thought, "I'm dying to know what happens next"? A writer should use conflicts to keep the story's engine humming so the reader is compelled to keep reading.

When you introduce a conflict, you should start by giving some background information. Let the reader know how and why the conflict started. For example, why are the two characters mad at each other? What are the rules of society that are causing the problem? What solutions to the problem is the character considering?

Overcoming a conflict is a popular theme that runs through different genres. In a folktale, a prince might slay the dragon, or a girl might succeed despite her evil stepmother. In a biography, a slave might find freedom, a boy who does not make the high school team might become a sports superstar, or a girl whose interest in computers is made fun of may grow up to own a successful company. In a science fiction narrative, a group of students may challenge a band of robots that took over the school, or a boy might come face-to-face with his own clone. In a realistic narrative, a boy might be caught in a shark attack, a girl might face her chief rival on the tennis court, or a boy may have to cope with his parents' divorce.

When you write your narrative, be sure to include at least one conflict. Give your main character a problem to overcome, and try to make the reader eager to find out how he or she handles it. A strong conflict makes for a strong narrative—and a reason to keep reading.

Point of View

A writer has choices when deciding which of the characters will tell the story. This gives the narrative its point of view. In other words, the character who tells the story is the person who has the point of view, like a lens through which the reader experiences the action. Imagine writing a story about a boy who has been ordered to clean his messy room. Think about the story being told from his point of view. Now think about the story being told from his mother's point of view. You can see how point of view can make a huge difference!

The character who tells the story expresses what he or she sees and thinks. Since different people have different viewpoints, your choice of who tells the story is an important one.

In a narrative, the writer usually uses one of two kinds of point of view: first-person or third-person. In first-person point of view, the story is told by one of the characters. The character uses "I" and "me."

From my point of view, this room looks perfectly fine! Why would Mom think there is anything wrong?

For example:

"I dare you," I said. I watched Jared pick up the worm. "I can't believe he will really do it," I thought. But he popped it into his mouth and smiled at me.

In third-person point of view, the story is told by someone outside the story. The writer uses the words "he," "she" and "they." These words show the actions and feelings of different characters. For example:

"I dare you," said Tate. He watched as Jared picked up the worm. "I can't believe you will really do it," Tate thought. But Jared popped it into his mouth. And smiled at Tate.

Most narratives can be told from a first- or third-person point of view. However, a personal narrative must be written from the first-person point of view. When you write a personal narrative, you use "I" to tell the story. You write about your own thoughts, feelings, and experiences. The reader learns the story through your eyes.

When you prepare to write your narrative, you should think about the point of view. Think how the story would go from the point of view of different characters. And you do not have to limit yourself to people. Narratives have been told from the point of view of an animal and even an inanimate object, like a rock.

Theme

What are you writing about?

All narratives have a theme. The theme is the main idea and the lesson the reader learns from the story. The theme can often be summed up in one sentence. Proverbs are often themes. A proverb is a saying that holds a truth. "Don't put all of your eggs in one basket" is an example of a proverb.

Some narratives may have more than one theme. The theme is not usually obvious at first. Some common themes deal with success, love, and courage.

When you write a narrative, it can help to think of the theme of the book before you start. Ask yourself, "What lesson do I want the reader to learn from the story?" Make it a point to make the reader work a little to find it out.

Themes:

Here are examples of themes in different genres of narratives:

Adventure. One theme of *Julie and the Wolves* by Jean Craighead George—"Growth comes from surviving challenges."

Fantasy. *A Wrinkle in Time* by Madeleine L'Engle—"The power of love is stronger than the power of evil."

Historical narrative. *No Hero for the Kaiser* by Rudolf Frank—"It sometimes takes more courage not to fight than to fight."

Humor. *Green Eggs and Ham* by Dr. Seuss—"You don't know whether you like it if you don't try it."

Multicultural. *Dragonwings* by Lawrence Yep—"Prejudice can cause conflict and strong emotions."

Mystery. *Encyclopedia Brown Tracks Them Down* by Donald J. Sobol—"Mysteries can be solved by paying attention and being persistent."

Realistic. *Bridge to Terabithia* by Katherine Paterson—"Being different can be difficult."

Science fiction. *Star Wars* by George Lucas—"Good triumphs over evil."

Sports. *Off* by Matt Christopher—"Overcoming fears will help you become your best."

✓Dialogue

Dialogue is conversation between characters. It is found in most, but not all, narratives. Dialogue should sound natural, as if the characters were really talking.

Dialogue is usually written in quotation marks. "The quotation marks let you know someone is talking," said Joe. A narrative should not only be made up of dialogue, however. Action and description should also be included.

Dialogue is used for different and important reasons in a narrative. Dialogue can:

- Reveal the personality of the speaker
- Reveal the personality of characters around the speaker
- Show the mood of the speaker
- Give the reader facts
- Move the action of the plot forward
- Build suspense

When you write dialogue, it is important to stay true to each character's personality and background. You should consider:

Age. How old the character is helps determine what words he or she will use. A two-year-old might say "I go potty!" But it is likely this dialogue would be different if it came from your teacher.

Where he or she lives. People from different areas of the country have different ways of speaking. For example, when talking to several people, someone from the South might use the word "y'all." A teenager from another region might say "You guys."

Whom he or she is talking to. A character will choose different words when he or she is talking to different people. For example, a boy will probably be more formal when he is talking to the principal than when he is talking to his friends.

Form of communication. Dialogue can be made up of characters speaking. Yet characters also can communicate in other ways. They can write or e-mail each other. For example, a dialogue in e-mail might be: "Sup?" "IM bored." "Me 2." "BBFN." "TTYL."

Mood. How the character is feeling is often expressed through dialogue. For example, we see the excitement of this character through her dialogue: "I can't believe I won front-row tickets to a concert by my favorite group!"

When you write dialogue, remember that the dialogue is supposed to sound natural. Pretend you really are the character who is talking. Saying the words in the dialogue out loud after you write them can help. Then you can see if any of the words sound out of place or if you are right on target. Also, observe conversation. Do people really listen to each other?

Figurative Language

Figurative language can be used to create vivid descriptions in narrative writing. Figurative language uses words that compare, exaggerate, or mean

Kinds of figurative language:

Simile. A comparison between two things using "like" or "as":

> The lump on my head is as hard as a rock.
> His hair was like straw.

Metaphor. A comparison between two things without using "like" or "as":

> The sunset is a crimson stripe in the sky.
> Their taunts were knives thrown at her heart.

Hyperbole. A large exaggeration:

> I'm so hungry I could eat a horse.
> That ghost story made my skin crawl.

Personification. Giving nonhumans human qualities:

> The dog gave her a dirty look and slunk away.
> Mother Nature sent a message that day.

Irony. Saying the opposite of what is meant:

> I flunked the test; that's just great.
> We're zero for ten; we'll be state champions for sure.

Onomotopoeia. A word that sounds like what it means:

> The doorbell buzzed even louder.
> She splashed into the pool.

something different from what they seem to mean. It helps the reader create a picture in his or her mind.

The opposite is literal language, which is saying what you mean. If you said, "He jumps very high," you would be using literal language. But if you say, "He jumps so high he is going to land on the moon!" you are using figurative language.

Have you ever heard anyone say, "It's just a figure of speech"? That is another term for figurative language.

Given the opportunity, young writers are often better at figurative language than adult writers because of their imaginations. They see things in new ways, with fresh eyes.

Figurative language can add to the quality of your narrative. The words are more memorable. The writing is simply more fun.

But there is a form of figurative language that should be limited: the cliché. A cliché is an expression that has been used so much it is worn out. Examples include: "Don't put off until tomorrow what you can get done today!" and "It's raining cats and dogs!"

Instead of using clichés, be original. Think of new figures of speech to add interest to your narrative writing.

Flashback and Foreshadowing

A flashback takes the reader back in time. A flashback can provide background information about the past, or it can show a memory and what a character has gone through. After a flashback ends, the story continues where it left off.

Foreshadowing is used to prepare the reader for future events. Foreshadowing can drop a hint about what is going to happen to make the reader interested to read more. For example, a story might have a new student enter the class and sit near the main character. He does not say or do anything—yet. But we know the author added the character for a reason. We will just have to wait and see what the reason will be.

Chapter Four

Prewriting

So you know the elements of a narrative. Now you should write, right? Wrong. Your first step is called *prewriting*. Prewriting is a stage that should not be skipped. In the prewriting stage you decide what you want to say and plan and organize your ideas. Then you consider how it will be said. You may want to collect ideas and information that you may be including in your narrative. Sometimes writers like to use *freewriting*. Freewriting is a process where you write your thoughts, feelings, and ideas without preparing too much beforehand. Freewriting allows you to express yourself creatively and get into the writing "flow."

Getting ideas:

One of the most common questions people ask authors is, "Where do you get your ideas?" Here are some suggestions:

1. **Keep a journal.** Reading a diary later can help you remember interesting people and events.

2. **Brainstorm.** Write down as many ideas as you can think of, as fast as you can. Evaluate them after you are done to see which will make the best narrative.

3. **Talk to people.** Ask questions about their experiences, their opinions, their feelings. Even those you think you know well may surprise you!

4. **Take notes.** Keep a pad and pencil with you at all times to jot down ideas.

5. **Read the newspaper.** Current events and human interest stories may provide a springboard for your own ideas.

6. **Ask yourself questions.** What if . . . ? Just suppose . . . ? Why is . . . ? The answers may turn into a story!

Choosing a Topic

How do you choose your topic? If you are writing a narrative for school, you might have been assigned a topic. But you might be able to choose any topic you want. Think about a topic that interests you. Have you ever read a story and thought, "Wow, the author really is into this subject"? Chances are, you were more interested in it too! Try to choose a topic you want to learn more about or share with others. The topic is the main subject of the narrative.

Type of Narrative

Consider which kind of narrative you want to write. If you are writing a personal narrative, you will need to choose a topic that you have experienced. If you are writing nonfiction, you will choose a topic that is real. If you are writing fiction, the only limit is your imagination.

If a particular topic does not come to mind, try making a list. Just write anything down in which you have an interest. Do not worry yet about whether it will make a good narrative. Just let your thoughts spill out on the paper. Now, check through your

Don't disturb me! I'm trying to brainstorm.

Once upon a time . . .

Remember to check the focus of your topic!

list. Decide if the topic would work for your narrative. Do you want to write about a topic you already know, or do you plan to research?

Check the focus of your topic. If it is too general, there will be too much information to include. For example, the solar system might be too broad a topic. Instead, you could focus on one planet. On the other hand, if the topic is too narrow or specific, there will not be enough information for your narrative.

Consider which genres would work best with your topic. For example, if your topic is inline skating, you might write a sports story about a person who skates. However, you also might write a mystery solved by a boy who roller skates to the rescue, or a biography about a champion rollerskater, or a science fiction story about a planet where aliens have rollerskates instead of ears. One of the best parts of writing a narrative is being creative and original.

So let's review: When you prepare to write a narrative, ask yourself if the topic interests you. Will it interest others? Is there a clear focus that is not too general or specific? Does it fit the genre you would like to write? When you can answer yes to these questions, you are ready to go.

Title

After you have chosen your topic, you can create a title. This title might be changed later, but it will get you started in the right direction.

Titles can help give the reader an idea of what the topic will be. Consider these titles: *The Moons of Jupiter*, *Alien Rollerblade-Ears*, *Our Hike Up High Mountain*. However, not all titles need to tell the topic right away, especially in fiction. For example, you have to start the story before you know what the titles *Cinderella* and *How the Grinch Stole Christmas* mean.

Researching

If your topic requires research, the prewriting stage is the time to do it. Gathering information about your topic helps you know what to write. There are many sources for gathering research.

A *primary source* is an eyewitness account or original document. Primary sources include diaries, letters, and actual documents. People's words also can be primary sources, such as an interview with an expert on the topic.

Can I help?

Doing research is like playing detective, searching out facts and details that you need.

A *secondary source* is information that is taken from another source created through research. Books, magazines, and the Internet are secondary sources.

Where can you find research information? One place to start is the library. A library's research section contains books, journals, magazines, microfilm, and videos. Librarians are available to help with the process.

Another place to find research material is the Internet. The advantage of using the Internet is that it often is convenient and fast. The research might pop up in a matter of seconds. There might be many sources of information on the Internet. The risk is that it can be difficult to know if a source is reliable. Some Web sites give false information. Be sure to evaluate

Choosing the best sources:

How do you choose the best sources of information? You need to evaluate each source. Ask yourself these questions:

✔ Does the source give the information I need?

✔ Is the information up to date?

✔ Is the author or publication reliable?

If the answers are yes, the source is a good one to use.

who runs the Web site and has posted the information before you use it.

Graphic Organizers

It is a good idea to use a graphic organizer to organize your information. Think of a graphic organizer as a map that will help you stay on course. Graphic organizers can be used for nonfiction and fiction. Two types of graphic organizers you might use are outlines and story maps.

Outlining

An outline shows the main ideas and the supporting details. Think of it as a table of contents for your story. The main ideas are written next to Roman numerals. The details that support the main ideas are written next to capital letters. It will look like this:

I. Main Idea
   A. Supporting detail
   B. Supporting detail
II. Main Idea
   A. Supporting detail
      . . . and so forth

To start an outline, write down your main topics first. Here is an example:

I. I discover the alien.
II. I make friends with the alien.
III. I teach the alien to appreciate her rollerblade-ears.

Then, fill in the subtopics:

I. I discover the alien.
  A. I am in bed and hear a noise outside.
  B. A green face with rollerblades for ears stares at me.
  C. The alien is crying.

II. I make friends with the alien.
  A. I invite her in.
  B. I make her a glass of chocolate milk.
  C. She tells me she is an outcast from her planet because the other aliens have skateboards for ears.

III. I teach the alien to appreciate her rollerblade-ears.
  A. I tell the alien that skateboards are out and rollerblades are better.
  B. I grab my blades and show her how they work.
  C. I teach her to use her own ears, and she goes home to her planet happy.
  D. The next night, another alien peeks in my window. He has a scooter sticking out of his head.

Story Mapping

A story map shows how ideas fit into a narrative. It gives the main ideas of the different parts of the story. It can help organize the story to make it easier to write.

Here is an example of a story map.

Title. The Disaster of a Camping Trip

Author. Adam Samuel

Main Character. Me

Supporting Characters. Nate, Max, Max's friends

Conflict. Nate and I vs. Max and friends

Setting. The woods behind Nate's house

Rising Action.

    Event 1. Nate and I pitch the tent and get in our sleeping bags.

    Event 2. We are eating a bag of trail mix when we hear a noise.

    Event 3. A squirrel appears at the door of the tent. We name him Max and chase him away.

Climax. Max and five hundred of his closest friends suddenly swarm the tent, jumping on the top until it collapses. Throwing trail mix at the squirrels, Nate and I make a break for the house, not looking back until we are safely inside.

Resolution. The campout is moved to a new location: Nate's basement.

Hey! These prewriting steps will get me where I want to go!

Sequencing

Sequencing is determining the steps in the story as demonstrated in the outline and story map examples. In a narrative, you have to go through a sequence of events. First, this happens. Then, the next thing happens. This helps the reader follow the action from start to finish. Tell the story in the order that it happened (unless you use the flashback technique).

Chapter Five

It's Time to Write!

It is time to put your outline and your knowledge to use. Get out your pen and paper (or your computer) and get ready to write.

Rough Draft

Drafting is the process of putting words down on paper. Drafting connects the facts and ideas together. The first draft is also called the rough draft. This is the first try at writing a narrative. A writer uses a rough draft to get the ideas down without worrying about the exact words. You can follow the outline, but you might choose to change it once you start writing. Mistakes are to be expected in a rough draft. The goal of a rough draft is not to be perfect but to get started.

Write down all of your ideas and play with them to see what works best. If you think of an idea you like better, then make the change. Write the narrative from start to finish.

You might choose to write several more drafts before you are finished. These drafts are called revisions. Some writers find that they write drafts better if they leave time in between them. Then, when they read the draft, the story is fresh. They look at it a whole new way. It might seem boring to have to rewrite and make changes, but it can be the most fun part of the process. Think of it this way: You have gotten the outline and the research out of the way. Now your job is to make it the best story you can.

Boy, I have a lot of revisions to my rough draft!

Writing Skills

In the final stages, every writer needs to proofread. Here is where rules should apply. Check punctuation, spelling, sentence structure, and grammar. These are the tools that make the story work. It is the proper use of language that brings the story to life.

Sentence Structure

A sentence is a word or group of words that forms

a complete unit. A sentence needs a subject and a predicate. A subject names someone or something. A predicate gives information about the subject. For example, in the sentence "The superhero flew away," "superhero" is the subject and "flew away" is the predicate.

A simple sentence has one subject and one predicate. It has just one independent clause that gives one complete thought—for example, "He jumped." A simple sentence may have a compound, or plural, subject or a compound predicate. For example, "My sister and I wore bathing suits and flippers" has both a compound subject and a compound predicate.

A compound sentence is made up of two or more simple sentences. If they are joined by a conjunction, they are separated by a comma (for example, "David hit the ball, but the outfielder caught it"). If the simple sentences are not joined by a conjunction, they are separated by a semicolon (for example, "David hit the ball; Anne caught it").

A writer should avoid incomplete sentences and run-on sentences. An incomplete sentence is a fragment, or piece of a sentence. A run-on sentence has too many subjects or predicates. For example, "My mom left the school I thought she forgot me" is a run-on sentence. However, sometimes writers may need to "break the rules" when writing dialogue or the thoughts of a character. After all, people don't always speak or think in complete sentences!

Grammar

The subject goes with a verb. A verb is a word that shows action. The subject and verb should be in the proper tense—past, present or future. Here is an example of a sentence using the wrong tense: "I type this yesterday." (The sentence should read: "I typed this yesterday.")

Parts of speech:

Part of speech	What does it do?	Examples
Noun	Names something	Douglas, city, job, fear, cow, time, plant
Verb	Expresses action or state of being	dance, seem, look, drive, pedal, appear
Pronoun	Replaces nouns	I, me, mine, her, hers, us, we, ours, its, they, theirs, who, which
Adjective	Describes nouns or pronouns	red, beautiful, gross, slimy, fast, hot, tasty
Adverb	Tells when, where, or how	downstairs, yesterday, loudly, away, later, backward, rapidly
Preposition	Shows the relationship between a noun and another word	about, behind, down, for, into, near, of, on, through
Conjunction	Connects words	and, but, or, so, because
Interjection	Expresses strong feeling	wow, hooray, fantastic, absolutely

The subject and verb must agree in number. If the subject is singular, the verb is singular. If the subject is plural, the verb is plural. An example of incorrect number agreement is: "The baby swim in the pool with her father." (The sentence should read: "The baby swims in the pool with her father.")

Sentence Type

A narrative is made up of many sentences. There are several different kinds of sentences.

1. Declarative sentence

A sentence that makes a statement about a person, place, or thing.

> "The runner won the race in the final seconds."
>
> "The dog barked."

2. Interrogative sentence

A sentence that asks a question.

> "Did you see that?"
>
> "What color should I wear?"

Hmm . . . Maybe I should check my grammar?

Me likes to right narratives

3. Imperative sentence

A sentence that commands. (The subject often is not given in the sentence.)

> "Watch out!"
>
> "Clean up your mess."

4. Exclamatory sentence

A sentence that shows strong emotions.

> "I can't believe it!"

When you write a narrative, it might seem that thinking about grammar and rules of language is somewhat annoying. It is true that the creative part of writing can tend to be more fun than following the rules. Yet, following the rules of language can result in a story that is clearer and more readable. This ends up making the narrative more enjoyable for the reader.

Editing and Proofreading

Editing is making changes to help turn writing into a finished work. Proofreading is checking spelling, capitalization, grammar, word use, and punctuation. You will need to edit and proofread your rough draft. You might choose to have someone else look over your narrative to check for errors. This is called "having a second pair of eyes." It is easy to overlook mistakes in your own writing. Another person can see your writing with a fresh point of view and notice things you missed.

The Final Draft

You have written the narrative. You have edited and proofread. Now you are ready for the final draft. This will be the final version. It will be the one you turn in to your teacher, share with others, and present, saying, "This is my story!"

If you are handwriting your narrative, you can transfer the edits from the rough draft to clean paper. Use your best handwriting. If you are writing on the computer, you can delete, retype, and edit directly on the screen.

Proofreader's marks:

Proofreaders use certain marks on rough drafts.
The marks are shorthand so the writer quickly
knows what needs to be fixed.

Proofreader's Mark	What it Means	Example
∧	Insert (put in)	It was a chocolate cookie.
ℛ	Delete (take out)	He laughed ~~laughed~~ aloud.
≡	Capitalize	julie wrote it.
/	Make lowercase	VeRy Funny.
⌒	Close space	It was mag ical.
#	Add a space	Jane went out.
∿	Transpose	My odg slept.
(SP)	Spell out	She's 16 today.
⊙	Add a period	The end
∧	Add a comma	Joe Sue, and Fred talked.
⌄	Add an apostrophe	The dogs collar is loose.
⌄⌄	Add quotation marks	Wow! she yelled.
⌃⌄	Add a semicolon	He coughed we all jumped.
ɟ / ɟ	Add parentheses	Her brother known as Spike is here.
¶	Start a new paragraph	She stopped. Meanwhile, back at the ranch,

Make your final draft as clean and close to perfect as possible. If your story is full of errors or is hard to read, the reader will not enjoy it as much. Plus, having a clean final draft shows off all of your hard work.

Checklist for editing:

- ✔ Do the words make sense?
- ✔ Are the words spelled correctly?
- ✔ Would another word be a better choice?
- ✔ Did you use complete sentences?
- ✔ Did you avoid run-on sentences?
- ✔ Do the subjects and verbs match?
- ✔ Is the punctuation correct?
- ✔ Does the action flow?
- ✔ Do the characters stay in character?
- ✔ Does the story accomplish your goal?
- ✔ Is the story interesting to read?
- ✔ Is there anything you still want to change?

Chapter Six

Share It and Publish It

The final step of the writing process is publishing. During this step, you share the final draft with other people.

You might take a personal approach with your writing. Share your work with your friends and family. It can be very rewarding when they enjoy what you have written. They might offer suggestions to make your work even better.

You might share your work in class. If your narrative is a school assignment, you might have to turn it in to a teacher. You also might share your writing with other students by copying it for a handout or reading it aloud to the class. You might hang it on the bulletin board or leave it in a shared reading space.

If you have written for younger children, you might read your story aloud to a school class.

Presentation

How your story looks may not seem important. The story is only about the words, isn't it? Or is it? Consider how you decide what to read. You look at the cover of a book or the magazine to see if it "looks good," right? If your work is presented well it will be more appealing to readers. It will also show your pride in your work.

You might choose to add graphic design to your story. If you have a computer, you can choose from different ways to design. You can play with fonts to match the style of your narrative. You can add graphics and color. You can easily print many copies to share.

Appearance counts! Don't turn in a sloppy narrative!

Oops . . .

Even if you do not use a computer, you can make your story look appealing with design. Neat handwriting helps. You can design a cover and make it into a book. If you are interested in art, you can add illustrations you draw yourself.

Becoming a Published Author

Wouldn't it be thrilling to see your name on a story in a magazine or newspaper or on the cover of a published book? There are many places for young people to have their writing published. If your work is chosen, you will be a published author. You might win prizes or even get paid for your work.

So you want to try to be a published author? Go for it! There are many places you can submit your narrative. Do not get discouraged if your work is rejected. Every published author has experienced a rejection at one time or another (and some experience many). Keep trying. Get feedback from your teachers or adults on how to improve your chances. Here are some submission possibilities:

School newspaper. Your school newspaper is a great place to start. Talk to the editor or the newspaper advisor to find out how to submit your writing.

Local newspaper. If your story is nonfiction and has local interest, submit it to a newspaper. You will want to find out the name of the appropriate editor. Different editors handle different sections, such as local news, gardening, and sports. Look in the paper to see which editor fits your story best.

Magazine. Many magazines accept work from freelance writers. To freelance means to work for yourself.

Web sites. Opportunities to get your writing published online abound. There are Web sites for every topic, including the one you have written about. Get permission from your parents before you search the Internet and submit anything. Do not give out your name and address unless your parents have given permission.

Contests. Many writing contests are open to young people. Some offer prizes, money, or the chance to be featured in a publication.

Publishing companies. Most publishing companies focus on publishing books written by adults. However, a few publish works written by children. In fact, some of these companies publish only children's works. Others have a few young authors in their mix. Look up books that are published by young people. Find out the companies that publish them. You will need to find out the name of the person who reads submissions. There are strict guidelines

Extra! Extra! Read all about my great article!

Wow! This is really good!

Main Street USA

to follow to submit work to a publisher. Read a book or article on how to prepare your work to submit. It is very difficult to get chosen by a publisher, but you may just be the one to do it!

Writing a Query Letter

Suppose you want to get your writing published. A query letter can be a helpful tool. A query letter is a letter introducing your writing in a way that hooks the reader. The person you send it to might want to

Dear Editor:

She has appeared in more than 150 plays around the country. She has worked with celebrities and has funny stories to tell about them. Our town is going to recognize her work by naming a street after her. She is my aunt.

In my article "My Aunt, the Street," I will interview my aunt about how she feels about being able to drive down a street with her name on it. I also interviewed a movie star she worked with who told me about the practical jokes they played on each other.

Please let me know if you would like to publish the enclosed article.

Sincerely,
Julie Quinn

Don't make your query dreary! Be a cheerleader for your own work and motivate others to want to read it!

know what the story is about before having to read the whole thing. You want the person reading the letter to be so excited that he or she cannot wait to read the story. A good query letter can be as much fun to read as the narrative. See the example on the previous page.

You Did It!

Congratulations! You have worked through each step of the writing process and met your goal. You have written a narrative. Narrative writing takes effort, but as you have learned, it can also be a lot of fun. Your finished narrative has captured your thoughts, feelings, and ideas in written form. Pat yourself on the back and share your work with pride. You did it!

Wrap-up

How did your story turn out? Are you satisfied with what you wrote? Review this list to evaluate your narrative writing:

1. Are you satisfied with the title?
2. Is there a clear theme?
3. Does the introduction draw the reader in?
4. Is the language vivid, creating images in the readers' minds?
5. Do the characters seem real?
6. Is the narrative well-organized?
7. Is there a conflict or conflicts?
8. Is there a satisfying ending?
9. Are the punctuation, grammar, and spelling correct?
10. Do you think it is a good story?

Good job!

We did it!

Steps in the Narrative Writing Process

Prewriting

- ✔ Select your topic
- ✔ Choose type of narrative and genre
- ✔ Do research if necessary
- ✔ Make an outline or story map

Writing

- ✔ Do a rough draft
- ✔ Revise, edit, and proofread
- ✔ Do a final draft

Publishing

- ✔ Turn it in to your teacher
- ✔ Present it to an audience
- ✔ Submit it for publication

Glossary

action—The movement in a story.

body—The main part of a piece of writing, after the lead and before the conclusion.

brainstorming—Producing a number of ideas to be evaluated later.

character—A person, animal, or other creature in a narrative.

climax—The high point or turning point in a story.

conflict—Struggle or problem.

dialogue—Conversation between characters.

draft—A version of a piece of writing.

exposition—The beginning of a story, introducing the characters, setting, and problem.

figurative language—Words used to convey a mood or feeling in a creative way.

flashback—Looking back at events that happened at an earlier time.

foreshadowing—Hinting at events to come.

freewriting—Writing down thoughts, feelings, and ideas without much preparation or revision.

introduction—The beginning of a piece of writing.

narrative—Another word for story; can be either fiction or nonfiction.

plot—The main events that take place in a narrative.

point of view—The view from which a story is told.

prewriting—The stage of planning and organizing before the actual writing.

resolution—The ending of a narrative.

sequencing—Putting the steps of a story in the correct order.

theme—The statement or lesson a narrative is trying to express.

topic—The main idea or subject.

Further Reading

Hanley, Victoria. *Seize The Story*: *A Handbook for Teens Who Like to Write*. Fort Collins, Colorado: Cottonwood Press, 2008.

Kamberg, Mary-Lane. *The I Love To Write Book: Ideas and Tips for Young Writers*. Milwaukee, Wisconsin: Crickhollow Books, 2008.

Mazer, Ann *Spilling Ink: A Young Writers Handbook*. New York: Roaring Book Press, 2010.

Internet Addresses

KidsCom—Write Me a Story
<http://www.kidscom.com/create/write/write.html>

Amazing Kids! Contests
<http://mag.amazing-kids.org/contests/amazing-kids-contests/>

Index